reaching out to

THE METHODISTS

*with heart
and mind*

William J. Whalen

LIGUORI
PUBLICATIONS

One Liguori Drive
Liguori, Missouri 63057
(314) 464-2500

Imprimi Potest:
John F. Dowd, C.SS.R.
Provincial, St. Louis Province
Redemptorist Fathers

Imprimatur:
+ Edward J. O'Donnell
Vicar General, Archdiocese of St. Louis

ISBN 0-89243-207-1

Excerpts from *Vatican Council II: The Conciliar and Post Conciliar Documents,* edited by Austin Flannery, O.P., copyright 1975, used by permission of Costello Publishing Co., Northport, New York 11768.

Table of Contents

1. A Not Unfamiliar Spirit

By any standards, the founder of the Methodist movement was a remarkable Christian. Had John Wesley been born a Catholic instead of an Anglican, he probably would have launched a revival such as that of Saint Francis of Assisi, or perhaps he would have founded a religious order. In fact, Methodism sought to recapture Catholic elements hidden by the Calvinist orientation of the Anglican establishment.

Wesley and his companions started a revival movement which was essentially carried on by lay people. They organized Bible classes, preached to the common man who worked in the mines and factories and fields, and infused new life into the religious structures of their day.

Although both John and Charles Wesley were accused of being Jesuits in disguise and of subverting the Church of England, neither brother had much direct contact with Roman Catholicism, and they showed little sympathy for the Church of Rome. They never denied, however, that true Christians could be found in Roman Catholicism and every other Christian Church.

John Wesley, Methodism's chief founder, never intended his revival movement to develop into a separate Christian denomination. He declared, "I live and die a member of the Church of England and none who regard my judgment will ever separate from it." Those who were converted at Methodist meetings were expected to remain members of the Church of England or other Churches and to attend worship and receive Holy Communion in these churches. But the Established Church failed to understand the dynamics of Methodism and dismissed Wesley and the people called Methodists as mere enthusiasts. The particular circumstances of the American Revolution led to the break between Anglicanism and the Methodist societies in the New World.

In many respects, Methodism is well suited to the American temperament. Methodism has never been greatly concerned with theology or with heresy trials and excommunications. Its activist impulse has led the Church to found scores of colleges and universities, social agencies, and benevolent institutions. The Puritan tradition of colonial America is still reflected in Methodism's abhorrence of liquor, tobacco, and gambling. However, ministers no longer must pledge total abstinence.

As they practiced the virtues of sobriety, thrift, and industry, the Methodists improved their economic and social status. Methodist pews often filled with bank presidents, professors, industrialists, and businessmen; the factory worker and small farmer gravitated toward the Pentecostal and Holiness Churches.

Today the Methodists form the second largest body of Protestants in the United States.

The Catholic writer John Todd has observed: "A Catholic today would like to invite Methodists to turn more closely to the teaching of their founder; and Catholics, too, might well look more lovingly on one whose life and teachings correspond with the traditional Christian idea of sanctity" (*John Wesley and the Catholic Church*).

2. *Where They Come From*

A REJECTED REVIVAL OF ANGLICANISM

The established Church of England of the early eighteenth century desperately needed reform and renewal. Morals, church attendance, and evangelism had sunk to low levels. The workingman and his family rarely took any interest in the worship and life of the Anglican Church.

Into this situation came two remarkable brothers who sought to invigorate the lethargic Anglican Church of which they were priests.

The Wesley Brothers

John Wesley was born in an Anglican parsonage in Epworth (a village about 100 miles north of London) on June 17, 1703. His father was rector at Epworth. The greatest influence on John's life was his mother, Susanna. One of twenty-five children herself, she gave birth to nineteen children.

When John was only five, a fire in the rectory at Epworth almost took his life. His escape prompted his mother to call him "a brand plucked from the burning."

Susanna prescribed a stiff program of study for her children at home before they started formal schooling. John left for prep school at Charterhouse in London in 1714, and entered Oxford in 1720.

He was elected a Fellow at Lincoln College in 1726, which testified to his scholarship. So long as he remained a celibate, he would receive a stipend from the college. Ordained a deacon in the Church of England, Wesley went back to Epworth to assist his father as curate of the parish. He was ordained a priest in 1728. When he was summoned back to Lincoln College, he discovered that his brother Charles and several companions had started a small club aimed at furthering the personal holiness of its members.

Daily study of the Bible, weekly reception of Holy Communion, fasting, visitation of nearby prisons, and religious instruction of poor children were prescribed for club members. The Wesleys devoured the spiritual works of William Law, such as his "A Serious Call to a Devout and Holy Life" and "A Treatise on Christian Perfection." An important source of spiritual direction for Wesley throughout his life was *The Imitation of Christ* by Thomas à Kempis, a fifteenth-century German monk. Scoffing Oxonians called the members of the club "Bible Moths," "Holy Clubbers," and "Methodists" because of the methodical way of life they advocated.

This early Methodist society bore some resemblance to later Methodism, but the real character of Methodism would be molded later, after the scene had shifted from the serenity of Oxford to America and a primitive settlement colonized by debtors and prisoners.

Impact of Hus and Luther

General James Oglethorpe, organizer of the colony in Georgia, wanted a clergyman to minister to his settlers and possibly preach to the Indians. John volunteered, and Charles became the general's secretary. The brothers sailed for the New World in 1735. On board the ship John was particularly impressed by a band of Moravians from Germany, who seemed unperturbed by the raging storms and demonstrated a faith far more secure and confident than his own. These Moravians were the spiritual heirs of John Hus, the fifteenth-century Bohemian reformer who was burned at the stake.

The experience in Georgia was a fiasco. The Indians were not interested in the Gospel, and Wesley called them "gluttons, thieves, liars and murderers." John fell in love with an eighteen-year-old girl in the colony, but she married another man; perhaps in retaliation he denied her Holy Communion. His harsh religious discipline antagonized parishioners. In 1737 John Wesley sailed for England and judged his experience in America to be a failure. "I who went to America to convert others was never myself converted to God," he wrote.

A religious experience, a conversion, did take place in London later, and dramatically changed the direction of John Wesley's life. For some weeks he had been meeting with a band of Moravians in London. On May 24, 1738, he dropped into a Moravian meeting. He later described this experience:

In the evening I went very unwillingly to a society in Aldersgate Street, where one was reading Luther's *Preface to the Epistle to the Romans.* About a quarter before nine, while he was describing the change which God works in the heart through faith in Christ, I felt my heart strangely warmed. I felt I did trust in Christ, Christ alone, for salvation; and an assurance was given me, that he had taken away my sins, even mine, and saved me from the law of sin and death.

Societies for the Spiritually Elite

John Wesley was now thirty-five years old. He believed he had received an assurance of salvation that he had never known before. He, his brother, and a colleague, George Whitefield, began to preach to the common people wherever they found them. Their disregard of ecclesiastical proprieties antagonized many Anglican bishops and rectors. Most Anglican pulpits were closed to them, but they began to preach to enormous crowds in the fields or in available halls. Wesley's idea was to form societies of the spiritually elite within the Anglican Church; the sole requirement for membership was an expressed desire to "flee from the wrath to come, and be saved from sins." Wesley appointed lay preachers to supervise his societies, but he directed the Methodists to attend worship and receive the sacraments in their own churches.

While John was the indefatigable preacher and organizational genius of Methodism, Charles became its poet. Charles published more than 4,400 hymns, including "Hark, the Herald Angels Sing" and the Easter anthem "Christ the Lord Is Risen Today." The brothers collaborated for many years, but eventually became estranged.

Basic to Wesley's plan of evangelism was the organization of the class system. A dozen Methodists would gather each week for prayer, mutual confession, and Bible study. Each member would contribute one penny to advance the work of the society. This "cell" form of organization was later taken over by the trade unions and even the Communist Party, but it has practically disappeared in contemporary Methodism.

Some Anglican bishops considered Wesley and his preachers as interlopers. When one bishop accused Wesley of preaching without authorization in his diocese, Wesley replied: "All the world is my parish." During his lifetime he traveled more than 250,000 miles and delivered tens of thousands of sermons.

Perhaps the dominant influence of his mother handicapped John Wesley in his romantic life. We have seen the outcome of his love affair in Georgia. Later in life he fell in love with a widow, Grace Murray, but Charles interfered and she married another man. Finally, after a two-week courtship, John married a widow and mother of four, Mrs. Mary Vazeille, who turned out to be a shrew. They quit living together, and John did not even hear of her death until after the funeral.

Charles entered a happy marriage and engaged in less itinerant preaching than his brother. His son Samuel became a Roman Catholic at the age of eighteen, and was known as one of the foremost church organists in English history.

In 1769 Wesley sent two official missionaries to the colonies, but by this time there were already Methodist societies in existence from New York to Virginia.

In America, as in England, the Methodists were instructed to attend the local Anglican Churches and to receive Communion from ordained Church of England clergymen. But after the American Revolution (which John Wesley vehemently opposed), most of the Anglican clergy and many Methodist preachers returned to the mother country or fled to Canada. The Methodists had few to whom they could turn to receive the sacraments.

The Break

Wesley had tried unsuccessfully to get some of his lay preachers ordained by the Bishop of London. He finally came to the conclusion that a presbyter (priest) and bishop were the same thing; as a priest he began to ordain ministers for his societies. This action angered Charles, who held that John had usurped the power of the bishop; the brothers never agreed on this issue. Charles declared: "My brother has put an indelible stigma upon his name."

About sixty American Methodist preachers held a conference in December 1784 and elected Francis Asbury and Thomas Coke to be superintendents of the Church in the United States. Twelve other men were elected elders and empowered to administer Holy Communion. Soon afterward both Asbury and Coke assumed the title "bishop" over Wesley's protests. In a bitter letter to Asbury, Wesley wrote:

> How can you, how dare you, suffer yourself to be called Bishop? I shudder, I start at the very thought! Men may call me a knave or a fool, a rascal, a scoundrel, and I am content; but they shall never by my consent call me Bishop!

The Methodist Church in America had become an independent Christian Church, with its own bishops and ministers, churches and sacraments. The same path to independence would be followed in England, but only after John Wesley's death in 1791.

3. *Where They've Been*

THE AMERICAN EXPERIENCE

An Irish immigrant, Philip Embury, began the first Methodist society in America in 1766. In 1768, this congregation built the John Street Chapel, which is still standing in the Wall Street area of New York City.

The Circuit Riders

The man who did the most to plant Methodism firmly in American soil was Francis Asbury, a blacksmith turned preacher. He not only rode hundreds of thousands of miles himself and preached numerous sermons but also organized the amazingly successful circuit riders who brought Methodism to the frontiers. Asbury arose every day at 4:00 A.M.; while in the saddle he taught himself Latin, Greek, and Hebrew. When Asbury began his labors, he could count several thousand Methodists in the colonies; however, by the time he died in 1816 there were more than 200,000.

The circuit rider was the main reason why Methodism soon outstripped in numbers such denominations as the Presbyterian, Episcopalian, and Congregationalist, who had been in

America a century or more before the first Methodist preacher. These denominations clung to the Atlantic seaboard, and attempted to fill their pulpits with seminary-trained clergymen. Meanwhile, the Baptists and Methodists planted thousands of congregations in the western settlements and in the South.

The Methodist circuit rider traveled from one settlement to another. Like Asbury himself, most of these early circuit riders were celibate; at one time in the Virginia conference only three of the eighty-four preachers were married men. Many of these dedicated men burned themselves out before they were thirty years old. They carried a Bible and hymnal in their saddlebags, and set up classes among the frontiersmen according to the original Wesleyan pattern.

Racial-Religious Conflicts

Methodism in the United States did not escape schism. From its earliest days in the colonies, Methodism attracted blacks, both slave and free. At various times, groups of black Methodists, chaffing under discrimination, broke away to found separate black Churches.

Wesley and the early Methodists held strong anti-slavery positions. The 1784 conference voted to expel all slaveholding members and any who bought or sold slaves. However, over the years the stand against slavery was softened. Black Methodists were forced to sit in the balcony or in a separate section of the church and to receive Communion only after all the whites had received.

In 1787 a group of blacks withdrew from the Methodist Church in Philadelphia. They organized a separate Church, the African Methodist Episcopal Church, in 1816; the first bishop of this Church was consecrated by Asbury. Before the Civil War the AME Church was confined to northern states, but it now has congregations throughout the country. The members support foreign missions in Africa and the West Indies.

A group of blacks who protested racial discrimination in the John Street Church began the movement which led to formation of the African Methodist Episcopal Zion Church. Their first

Church, founded in 1800, was called Zion, and they added this to the name of the new denomination. The first annual conference was held in 1821. Missionaries have been sent to Liberia, Ghana, Nigeria, South America, and the West Indies.

Like most of the major Protestant denominations, Methodism was divided over the issue of slavery as well as of race. In Methodism the occasion for the schism was the argument over a bishop who had inherited slaves and who married a woman who also owned slaves. Church regulations forbade bishops and ministers from being slaveholders, but Georgia law forbade emancipation of slaves. Northern Methodists attacked the bishop, and Southerners defended him. The issue could not be resolved, and the Methodist Episcopal Church South was organized in 1845.

With the help and encouragement of white Methodists in the Methodist Episcopal Church South, a group of Negroes founded the Colored Methodist Episcopal Church in 1870. The name was changed to the Christian Methodist Episcopal Church in 1954.

Other Divisive Factors

Some Methodists who wanted more power for the laity organized the Methodist Protestant Church in Baltimore in 1830. Within eight years this Church had grown to 50,000 members.

Protesting slavery and episcopacy, a group of Methodists formed the Wesleyan Methodist Church in 1843. It united with the Pilgrim Holiness Church in 1968; the resulting body was named the Wesleyan Church. This Church in turn may merge with the Free Methodist Church. It reports 103,000 members in the United States.

The Free Methodists were founded by the Reverend B. T. Roberts, who objected to what he termed the liberalism and betrayal of true Wesleyanism by the larger Church. The first Free Methodist Church was organized in Pekin, New York, in 1860. This Church forbids membership in secret societies and demands adherence to strict moral standards. There are 68,000 members in the United States.

The Salvation Army

As eighteenth-century Anglicanism was unable to contain Methodism, so nineteenth-century Methodism was unable to contain the revival among the lower classes led by a fiery Methodist preacher, William Booth. As General Booth, he would found the Salvation Army, a semi-military Protestant Church dedicated to the evangelization of the workers and the poor.

4. *What They're Like*

HOLY ENTHUSIASM WED TO PRACTICALITY

Wesley assumed that the members of his Methodist societies would subscribe to the traditional beliefs of Protestant Christianity, but he did not impose dogmas. Accordingly, he wrote, "As to all opinions which do not strike at the root of Christianity, we think and let think." The United Methodist Church recognizes four main sources and guidelines for Christian theology: Scripture, tradition, experience, and reason. Today some Methodists stand in the fundamentalist tradition, while others hold a theology akin to Unitarianism.

Beliefs and Creed

The creed of the Methodist Church is the "Apostles' Creed," and it is usually recited at the Sunday worship service. Yet, to join a Methodist Church a convert need only affirm that Jesus Christ is the Son of God and everyone's personal Savior. The standards of doctrine are the twenty-five Articles of Religion, the fifty-two sermons of John Wesley, and *Notes on the New Testament* by Wesley. The day-to-day affairs of the Church are directed by the *Discipline,* a sort of code of canon law, which now covers 890 pages.

Wesley selected twenty-four articles from the thirty-nine Articles of Religion of the Church of England and sent these to the American societies for their adoption. To these twenty-four articles the American Methodists added one which recognized the independence of the colonies. These articles affirm belief in the Trinity, the Incarnation, the virgin birth, the Resurrection. The Bible is declared to contain all things necessary to salvation. Man is justified by faith and not works, but good works are the fruit of faith and are pleasing to God. There are only two sacraments: Baptism and the Lord's Supper. Purgatory and the veneration of saints and relics are condemned. The laity should receive both bread and wine in the Lord's Supper. (A regulation forbids the use of wine and substitutes unfermented grape juice.) A Mass for the dead is a "dangerous deceit."

Theology

Wesley's theology was essentially the theology of the Church of England, although he strongly opposed the Calvinistic doctrine of predestination held by some Anglicans. In this respect, he was an adherent of Arminianism, the modification of Calvinism taught by Jacobus Arminius (1560-1609), emphasizing freedom of the will and the belief that Jesus died for all men and not just the elect. Wesley preached that everyone could be saved, that man achieved justification by faith but that he could cooperate with grace and perform good works, that a Christian could be sure he was saved but might also fall from grace, and that a Christian could attain perfection in this life. His references to both Luther and Calvin were usually critical.

The doctrine of *perfection* or *entire sanctification* was Wesley's major contribution to Protestant theology. If a Christian could avoid sin for an hour or a day, he could achieve a state of perfection. Wesley never claimed that he had reached this state, but he presented it as an attainable goal for his followers. The Methodists then and now have paid particular attention to the action of the Holy Spirit in the Church and in the life of the individual believer.

Dr. Albert Outler, the distinguished Methodist theologian, has commented: "We (Methodists) classify ourselves as Protestants, but none of the classical traditions of continental Protestantism had anything like the Wesleyan ideal of 'Christian perfection' and the Wesleyan concept of evangelical morality" (*That the World May Believe*).

Worship, Prayer, and Fasting

The Lord's Supper is considered a memorial: "The body of Christ is given, taken, and eaten in the Supper, only after a heavenly and spiritual manner." A few Methodists believe in the Real Presence and hold a High Church view of the sacrament.

The Church practices infant baptism, but children do not become full members until they reach the age of ten or twelve. The form of baptism is considered of little importance; the *Discipline* authorizes baptism by sprinkling, pouring, or immersion.

Ministers preside at worship services wearing an academic gown, business suit, or alb and stole. An altar, cross, candles, and vested choir are common. A typical Sunday service includes several hymns, prayers, reading from the Scriptures, the Apostles' Creed, sermon, and offertory. Most congregations schedule Holy Communion once a month or once every quarter; the contemporary liturgical movement in Methodism appeals to Wesley's encouragement of frequent Communion to reestablish weekly Communion services.

Fasting played an important role in the Methodist movement as far back as its Oxford beginning, and Wesley warned that "the man who never fasts is no more in the way of salvation than the man who never prays." Like weekly Communion, the role of fasting in the believer's spiritual life was lost in most of American Methodism.

Few, if any, twentieth-century Methodists would qualify for membership in the original Oxford society. Among other things, those early Methodists were required to fast on Wednesdays and Fridays, spend at least two hours a day in prayer, and receive Holy Communion weekly.

Conduct and Discipline

Wesley's General Rules of conduct are published in every edition of the *Discipline.* Some of the admonitions warn the people called Methodists against blasphemy, fighting, usury, and self-indulgence. Others condemn buying or selling anything on Sunday and "putting on of gold and costly apparel."

Rule 3 of the General Rules is directed against "drunkenness, buying or selling spiritous liquors, or drinking them, unless in cases of extreme necessity." Methodism has always advocated total abstinence but no longer makes this a test of membership. Methodist interest in temperance is understandable when the degradation caused by liquor in Wesley's day is known. Wesley himself drank beer and wine but not hard liquor. The total abstinence movement within Methodism started only about 100 years ago; before that, temperance meant moderation in drink.

In 1873, in Ohio, a group of Methodist women knelt in front of saloons and prayed for an end of the liquor traffic. The next year they founded the Women's Christian Temperance Union (WCTU) which was led for many years by Frances Willard. Later, Methodist men founded the Anti-Saloon League. Carry Nation, the fiery prohibitionist who descended on many a saloon with hatchet in hand, belonged to the Free Methodist Church.

The Methodist Church takes credit for being one of the major forces behind the Eighteenth Amendment which brought prohibition to the United States. The Board of Temperance of the Church still lobbies for national prohibition, encourages local option prohibition, supports Alcoholics Anonymous, and asks young people to take the pledge on Commitment Sunday.

At one time Methodism frowned on dancing, card playing, the theater, circuses, and other diversions. Only some of the smaller Methodist sects still expect members to avoid these entertainments.

The Church endorses birth control. A recent General Conference declared: "We believe that planned parenthood, practiced in Christian conscience, may fulfill rather than violate the will of God." Like all denominations, Methodism deplores divorce but allows remarriage in cases such as desertion and adultery.

Church Organization and Structure

Methodism is highly organized. In fact, Methodism probably embraces more boards, committees, conferences, and other organizational units than any other Church. At the base of the pyramid is the local congregation which is known as a "charge." In the Methodist episcopal system the congregation does not hire or fire its minister. The ministers accept whatever charges are assigned by the bishop. This policy insures that every church has an appointed ministry and that all full-fledged ministers receive appointments. Methodism sees a rotating ministry as an advantage; thus Methodist ministers are shuffled around more often than the usual Protestant minister.

Groups of Methodist churches are organized in districts supervised by district superintendents. These districts correspond to rural deaneries in Catholicism. Superintendents are appointed by the bishop for one year terms for a maximum of six successive terms.

A Methodist bishop has charge of the churches belonging to a particular Annual Conference. Bishops are elected for life, but must retire at age seventy-two. This office carries with it no special spiritual powers, as it does in Roman Catholicism, Eastern Orthodoxy, and Anglicanism; but a Methodist bishop possesses considerable practical power. He appoints preachers, presides at conference meetings and, in general, oversees the spiritual and temporal welfare of the churches in his area.

At the apex of the pyramid is the General Conference which meets every four years. About 900 delegates, half of them ministers and half laymen, direct the overall policies of the Church. The General Conference can revise the *Discipline* of the Church, but it cannot change the twenty-five Articles of Religion or eliminate the episcopal form of Church government.

Methodism has always made good use of lay people. From the start of the movement, Wesley relied on lay preachers. Laity today participate in all of the governing conferences of the

United Methodist Church. More than 1,300,000 Methodist women belong to the Women's Society for Christian Service.

The Ministry

A young man (or woman) who feels called to Methodist ministry begins his career by going to the Quarterly Conference for a recommendation for a license to preach. If this is received, he applies to the district superintendent and a committee of five other ministers. They can authorize him as a "local preacher." The Church is under no obligation to provide local preachers with pulpits; these preachers usually support themselves in secular businesses and professions.

The next step for a local preacher is college (four years) and, probably, seminary training (three years). On completion of this educational preparation he may be received "on trial" as a traveling preacher. After two years in this category, he may be received in "full connection."

The Methodist Church recognizes two orders of the ministry: deacon and elder. A deacon can perform all the spiritual services within his own congregation, but he cannot administer Holy Communion outside of his congregation. An elder is ordained by the bishop and other elders and can function as a minister throughout the Church. The office of bishop is not a third office but an administrative position occupied by an elder.

Women have served Methodism as lay preachers from the very beginning, but it was not until 1956 that women were ordained as traveling preachers with full ecclesiastical rights. The Church also commissions deaconesses who work in hospitals and social agencies.

Methodism has no shortage of clergy, although not all ministers have college and seminary training. In fact, there are almost as many Methodist ministers in this country as there are priests who care for the 52 million Roman Catholics.

Good Works and Evangelism

More than 100 colleges and universities are related to the Church's board of education. Some connections are tenuous, and some — such as that with Vanderbilt and Southern California — have been broken; others, as those with Southern Methodist University, are solid. Methodists founded such institutions as Northwestern, Duke, Emory, DePauw, American, Ohio Wesleyan, and Oklahoma City. There are also a dozen Methodist seminaries with 3,400 men and women in training for the ministry.

The United Methodist Church operates, in Nashville, the nation's largest Protestant publishing house. The Board of Evangelism publishes *The Upper Room,* a devotional magazine popular among many Protestant denominations.

A strong missionary impulse has always motivated American Methodism. The Church supports missions in 48 countries with more than 600 missionaries and 4,200 ordained native ministers.

English Methodists hesitated to seek converts on the European continent. Conferences in the following countries are therefore related to American Methodism: Belgium, Austria, Czechoslovakia, Denmark, Finland, Sweden, Norway, Germany, Switzerland, and Hungary. These European conferences report about 145,000 members.

American Methodists have labored in India since 1856, and now count 152,000 full members and 250,000 preparatory members in West Pakistan. Korea has been a fruitful mission field; the 145,000 Korean Methodists worship in 1,230 churches and chapels.

Methodist missionaries in the Philippines minister to 73,000 adult members and 57,000 baptized children. The Methodist Church also seeks converts in ten Latin American countries.

Getting Acquainted

The average United Methodist congregation is small by Catholic standards — about 250 people. The average Catholic parish enrolls more than 1,800. The minister and parishioners are much more likely to know each other by name than in the typical Catholic parish, even though Methodist ministers are likely to change assignments every five or six years.

A Methodist who attends Mass will be able to recognize elements from his or her own worship service and vice versa. The introduction of the vernacular in the Mass and other liturgical reforms, as well as the gradual introduction of vestments, candles, and Church art into the Methodist churches, has facilitated the understanding of the respective worship services. Methodists do not practice devotion to the Blessed Virgin Mary or the saints.

Among the major Protestant denominations, many Methodists hold rather "liberal" views on such matters as abortion, divorce, and euthanasia, although some Methodists also support the Right to Life movement.

The worldwide character of the Roman Catholic Church contrasts with the predominantly American orientation of Methodism. The variety of nationalities and the range of incomes and education within American Catholicism points up the relative homogeneity of the United Methodist Church.

5. *Where They're Going Today*

THE SPIRIT CALLS TO UNITY

What began as a movement of spiritual renewal within the Church of England eventually became a separate Church: Methodism.

After Wesley's death, British Methodism broke away from Anglicanism and, then, divided into several groups such as the Methodist New Connection (formed in 1795), the Primitive Methodists (1807), and the Bible Christians (1815). Most British Methodists came together in a united Church in 1932. Unlike American Methodism, the English have never had bishops nor have they been preoccupied with the question of total abstinence. Membership in Methodist Churches in the British Isles has been declining — now standing at under 500,000 members — as has the number of ministers.

The American Scene

Methodism is primarily an American denomination and occupies a relatively minor niche in world Christianity. Of the estimated 1,100,000,000 Christians, only 20,000,000 or so belong to Methodist Churches. Of these, three out of four are Americans.

Unlike the Baptists, who remain divided into northern and southern Churches, the Methodists were able to reunite their Church. The union of the Methodist Episcopal Church, the Methodist Episcopal Church South, and the Methodist Protestant Church took place in 1939. This resulted in the formation of the Methodist Church, with a membership of nearly 11,000,000.

But their efforts at reconciliation have not stopped there. The Methodist Church united in 1968 with the Evangelical United Brethren, the Church which was itself formed by a union of two Churches in 1946. These were the Church of the United Brethren and the Evangelical Church, both founded by German-speaking Methodists.

These Churches originated in Pennsylvania in the early nineteenth century. When the Methodist bishops refused to incorporate German-speaking congregations into the Church, the founders established separate Churches which were Methodist in doctrine and practice. The EUB Church also retained traces of the Lutheran, Mennonite, and Reformed traditions of many of its early members. At the time of the 1968 merger, all but about 40,000 of its 750,000 members lived in the United States.

Today the largest Methodist body, the United Methodist Church, reports 9,500,000 members in 38,000 U.S. congregations, as well as 1,500,000 preparatory members and 500,000 in Europe, India, Africa, and the Philippines. About a third of these attend church on any particular Sunday. For more than a century it had been the largest Protestant Church in the country but that distinction has been yielded to the Southern Baptist Convention.

The Social Perspective

Most American Methodists come from English, German, and black backgrounds. Once the Church of the workingman, the United Methodist Church is thoroughly middle-class. Its adherents have succeeded in business, education, and politics; in a recent year more U.S. senators identified themselves as Methodists than Roman Catholics, although there are three or four Catholics for every Methodist in the population.

Three Methodists have occupied the White House: Grant, Hayes, and McKinley. Methodists are found in all walks of life: Mayor Tom Bradley of Los Angeles, Dallas Cowboys coach Tom Landry, Roberta Flack, Dionne Warwick, Senator John Tower, George Wallace, and Alistair Cooke of *Masterpiece Theater.* Probably the best-known Methodist minister, Oral Roberts, began his career in a small Pentecostal denomination but transferred to the United Methodist Church. The Methodist parsonage has been the boyhood home of many well-known Americans: Walter Mondale, George McGovern, David Frost, Mayor Harold Washington of Chicago, and Fran Tarkenton.

Since Methodism started in a university setting, Oxford, it may not be surprising that the Methodist Church founded more colleges and universities in this country than any other Protestant Church. Methodists also established more hospitals and homes for children and the aged than any other Church except the Catholic.

The Smaller Churches

About 4,000,000 Methodists in the U.S. belong to Churches other than the United Methodist Church. Most of these are blacks who worship in their own churches — the African Methodist Episcopal Church, the African Methodist Episcopal Church Zion, and the Christian Methodist Episcopal Church — with their own bishops and denominational organizations. A much smaller number of white Methodists belong to independent Methodist bodies.

Delegates to conventions of the AME Zion and the CME Churches have set 1985 as the target date for formulation of a plan for merger. In Japan, North and South India, and Canada, the Methodist Church has been absorbed into a larger united Protestant Church. For example, Canadian Methodists joined Congregationalists and Presbyterians in 1925 to form the United Church of Canada.

Ecumenism

Methodists have been involved in ecumenical developments from the start. A Methodist layman, Dr. John R. Mott, was instrumental in calling the World Missionary Conference at Edinburgh in 1910. This conference marked the start of the Protestant ecumenical movement. Mott later received the Nobel Peace Prize. The United Methodist Church, along with the major black Methodist bodies, belongs to the National Council of Churches and World Council of Churches.

John Wesley had little contact with Roman Catholicism and had some harsh words about Catholic beliefs, but he never displayed animosity toward Catholics as such. Some sections of the Methodist Church in this country may have vented anti-Catholic sentiments during the early decades of this century, but relations today between Catholics and Methodists are cordial.

Methodist observers, including Dr. Outler of Southern Methodist University, attended all sessions of the Second Vatican Council. Fruitful dialogues have been conducted in recent years by Methodists and Roman Catholics under official Church auspices.

At the 1968 General Conference, the United Methodist Church agreed to remove from its Articles of Religion "any derogatory references to the Roman Catholic Church."

Other Trends

A recent survey of adult Americans revealed that those who listed Methodism as their religious preference had dropped from fourteen percent of the population to only ten percent between 1967 and 1980.

Worldwide, the United Methodist Church reports 15,000,000 members, up 1,000,000 from ten years ago. This growth has come from mission areas in Africa and Indonesia.

Methodists do not hide the fact that their Church faces some serious problems. Membership in the United Methodist Church in the U.S. declined ten percent between 1972 and 1982; during the same decade the Southern Baptists grew by twenty percent.

Bishop Finis A. Crutchfield explains, "The average Methodist family has only 1.2 children per family. They're largely upper middle class and upper class, and they have fewer children, so we must reach out and evangelize."

6. *Where Do You Go from Here?*

Catholic theologians have come, in recent years, to a deep respect for the teaching of John Wesley on sanctification, seeing close resemblances to their own community's doctrine on grace. America's Catholic bishops have become spokesmen for a social gospel in basic harmony with that of the Methodists' founder who stated, "The Gospel of Christ knows no religion but social; no holiness but social holiness." And more and more rank-and-file Christians of both denominations are putting aside their few remaining vestiges of centuries-old animosity. The latter are not only joining forces to achieve peace with justice but also, as couples, committing their lives to Christian intimacy in the marital state. They find themselves called to do this regardless of painfully apparent institutionalized barriers still in place between their faith-support communities.

Such couples often find themselves at odds with the set policies of their Churches in the witness of their everyday lives or with the practices of their local officials. Sometimes, as a result of the ensuing battles, one or both spouses find themselves estranged from the communities through which the gift of faith came to them and through which it should be nourished.

What can such couples do? Contrary to the opinion of some, it is best that both members in such an interfaith union become more deeply involved with heart and mind in their respective Churches and more conversant with the wealth of their divergent traditions.

Such a practice need anticipate no compromise, no demeaning or conscience-disturbing admission, in practice or otherwise, that the doctrine of either Church is lacking in fullness. It will rather give expression to a simple and humble admission that the development of faith of the Christians engaged in dialogue is in progress, and a consequent eagerness on the part of both to share with each other the growth in faith that each gratefully accepts as gift.

In this sharing, interfaith couples should find reassurance in the words of Bishop J. Francis Stafford to the world synod of Catholic Bishops in 1980, in which he referred to interfaith marriages as "a special opportunity for Christian growth." He insists that such couples not be led "to ignore the real differences which exist in their faith orientation" but be encouraged to "search out and amplify areas of communality, truths on which they discover agreement and expressions of piety which bring both to a deeper awareness of God." The spokesman for the American bishops goes on to say, "What is behind this strategy is a belief in the authenticity of both faith orientations, if held in good conscience, and a hope that from their combination in the conjugal love, there will result a deeper marital union."

It goes without saying, of course, that if the non-Catholic partner feels called in his or her faith growth to join the Catholic Church, the Catholic partner will in no manner discourage him or her in this. This also is the intent of the Council fathers' respectful statement on *Religious Liberty* (3). "He is bound to follow this conscience faithfully in all his activity so that he may come to God, who is his last end. Therefore he must not be forced to act contrary to his conscience. Nor must he be prevented from acting according to his conscience, especially in religious matters."

We hope and pray that this booklet will help interfaith couples share the vision of faith. The absence of any kind of "discussion starters" is not an oversight; we felt that it would be presumptive, in matters so personal, to formulate the gifts that intimacy urges you to share.

Further Reading

Bucke, Emory, S. *The History of American Methodism.* Nashville, Abingdon, 1964.

Davies, Rupert E. *Methodism.* Baltimore, Penguin Books, 1963.

Ferguson, Charles W. *Organizing to Beat the Devil.* Garden City, New York, Doubleday, 1971.

Harmon, Nolan B. *Understanding the Methodist Church.* rev. ed. Nashville, Methodist Publishing House, 1961.

Lawless, Richard M. *When Love Unites the Church.* St. Meinrad, Indiana, Abbey Press, 1982.

Norwood, Frederick. *The Story of American Methodism.* Nashville, Abingdon, 1975.

Outler, Albert C. *John Wesley.* New York, Oxford University Press, 1964.

Richardson, Harry V. *Dark Salvation.* Garden City, New York, Anchor Press/Doubleday, 1976.

REACHING OUT WITH HEART AND MIND

A series of booklets that explore the history, beliefs, and traditions of the larger Christian Churches in the United States. $1.50 each.

Other booklets in this series from Liguori Publications include:

Reaching Out to THE LUTHERANS with Heart and Mind

Reaching Out to THE BAPTISTS with Heart and Mind

Reaching Out to THE PRESBYTERIANS and THE REFORMED with Heart and Mind

Reaching Out to THE EPISCOPALIANS with Heart and Mind

Order from your local bookstore or write to:
Liguori Publications, Box 060, Liguori, Missouri 63057
*(Please add 50¢ postage and handling for the first item
ordered and 25¢ for each additional item.)*